# Water/Music

Johns Hopkins: Poetry and Fiction

*Wyatt Prunty, General Editor*

OTHER BOOKS BY PETER FILKINS

POETRY

*What She Knew*

*After Homer*

*Augustine's Vision*

*The View We're Granted*

TRANSLATION

Ingeborg Bachmann

*Songs in Flight: Collected Poems*

*The Book of Franza & Requiem for Fanny Goldmann*

*Darkness Spoken: The Collected Poems*

Alois Hotschnig

*Leonardo's Hands*

Bernd Stiegler

*Traveling in Place: A History of Armchair Travel*

H. G. Adler

*The Journey*

*Panorama*

*The Wall*

BIOGRAPHY

*H. G. Adler: A Life in Many Worlds*

# Water/Music

Poems by PETER FILKINS

JOHNS HOPKINS UNIVERSITY PRESS
BALTIMORE

This book has been brought to publication
with the generous assistance of Darlene Bookoff
and the John T. Irwin Poetry and Fiction Endowed Fund.


Printed in the United States of America on acid-free paper
2 4 6 8 9 7 5 3 1

Johns Hopkins University Press
2715 North Charles Street
Baltimore, Maryland 21218-4363
www.press.jhu.edu

Library of Congress Cataloging-in-Publication Data

Names: Filkins, Peter, author.
Title: Water / music / poems by Peter Filkins.
Description: Baltimore : Johns Hopkins University Press, [2021] | Series: Johns Hopkins: poetry and fiction
Identifiers: LCCN 2020020194 | ISBN 9781421440088 (paperback) | ISBN 9781421440095 (ebook)
Subjects: LCGFT: Poetry.
Classification: LCC PS3556.I4288 W38 2021 | DDC 811/.54—dc23
LC record available at https://lccn.loc.gov/2020020194

A catalog record for this book is available from the British Library.



Johns Hopkins University Press uses environmentally friendly
book materials, including recycled text paper that is composed
of at least 30 percent post-consumer waste, whenever possible.

*for Leslie Kogod*

We take from nature what we cannot see.

We sigh before we sing.

Then almost silence, almost a pond-shimmer.

Theodore Roethke, from *Straw for the Fire: From the Notebooks of Theodore Roethke, 1943–1963*

# CONTENTS

## I



## II



## III

## IV



## V

# I

## IN VIVO

suffering knows
what cannot heal
the self embedded
in the pain of pain

and so continues
unrestrained
lancing the mind
that won't let go

the bloodied self
alone sustained
by sharper knowledge
suffering knows

# UTERINE VELLUM

on which the highest of the high
laws are wont to be inscribed,
laid out, set down, gone medieval
as the hide cut from an aborted calf,
pippined tight on a framing herse,
gobs of hair burned off by lime,
pumice pouncing to scud the rest

to creamy eloquence, calf veins
inveigling their flat gray cursive
through codexed neat beheadings,
marriages, deeds, and holy scripture
gilded, foliate as a eunuch's quaver:
"This stouffe we wrytte upon,
'tis made of beestis skynnes!"

# AUGUSTINE'S VISION

Many years later, while contemplating beauty
as order, he would think of them: gamecocks
digging in their claws for a scrap, and how
in the market's dusty tumult he felt compelled
to stop and watch them while on his way
to be baptized and confess himself a creature of sin.

Prisoner to his heart's regard, he courted error,
the beauty of a thing in and of itself
not always the same as God's invisible plan,
the gamecocks and their darting, skillful parries,
the exultant crowing, bodies taut with power,
soon whipping the crowd into a drunken frenzy.

"For what horizon do eyes of love not scan,
hoping for a hint of reason's beautiful scheme,"
he later wrote, thinking of savage birds
pitched in battle, pure animal action
without mind—limp wings and carriage, a croak
gone awry, all of it fitting nature's set way.

Though this was years before he lay on his deathbed,
Hippo surrounded, the Vandal hordes approaching,
himself lamenting his sins, remembering gamecocks,
their beaks and talons bloodied, no doubt convinced
a higher mind worked through them, ordering all things,
as the saint continued weeping inside his narrow cell.

# AUDEN'S GLASSES

Putting them on, one sees
dull history in stereo—
epics, wars, whole countries
transparent as a wish
wriggling in a petri dish,
and armies marching slow.

The ambivalent light of day,
the children quick to anger,
what one feels but cannot say
—all are obviously visible
as crosses on a hill
to the ignorant manger.

While buried in each scene
like a carpet's woven flaw,
the thread of a thread of a scream
interrupts the nuptials
staged as village miracles,
yet proving the hidden law:

That life is lived and suffered
in vain short-sighted views,
and the only solace offered
in the cell of the self alone
is to find it cannot atone
for what it knows, but cannot undo;

And failing that, soon cease
all claims to the quelling vision
that God begets Love begets Peace
in the belly of the End of Days,
and pour a drink, watch the fire raze
a tenement on television.

# THE HITLER BUG

Tell me, tell me please, that when Oscar Scheibel
dubbed a beetle *Anophthalmus hitleri* in 1937,
he could see his sick joke play out across history,
rabid neo-Nazis later spelunking the slimy caves
of Slovenia in search of "the eyeless Hitler,"
collectors forking out thousands for a blind bug
without notable features except a certain attraction

for exterminators, those right-wing extremists,
exigent, exacting, exultant, and extirpating
every last specimen, each exoskeleton
a blind and unwitting six-legged Führer
Scheibel thought a fool—O tell me!—
a monster worthy of the Valhalla of taxonomy,
cavernous extinction, the execrations of time.

# TRIPTYCH

## TO THE EMINENT HATE MONGERS

I, too, have wandered in the provinces
of blame, climbed the heady peaks of disdain
to breathe the bellicose air of mockery,
*they them you* and *us* the fertile seeds
of lush resentment sprouting its fruits and grains
in hothouses of malice, overheated incubators
oxygenating through the night the artificial
blossoms of fear, the fibrous roots of treachery.

Ah, such satisfaction. And how very sweet
the taste of dime-store righteousness. Who knew
it could feel this pleasurable? Whole counties
chugging sudsy drafts of smug, oak-aged
vintages of anger following hard on the heels
of those tasty distractions—bitterness
and spite, the flourishing and succulent
harvest of hate ripened on smears.

Yet remember, my friends, remember: Beware
the curse of language. Its deft perversions,
once unleashed, return always and ever
to eradicate all who consume them, poisoning
*you they them* and *us* until the very smell
of knowledge or conviction or simple decency
is enough to sicken, enough to cramp and roil
and retch whatever is left of the gutted truth

that will undo you, showing up one day
in the duchy of triumph, there inside the tower
of cynicism, at the resplendent ego's banquet
where softly afoot and on supple tawny hands
your heaping plates will be carried in, the cook
announcing with a smile as sharp and bright
as the grudge he harbors, "Ladies and gentlemen,
come to the table. It's time to eat your meal."

## SEVEN ALMONDS

Just to be alone
in the republic of thought,
no staff, no briefings.

Speeches, letters, notes.
Left hand curled in like a shield
or a scimitar.

Paris. Brussels. Nice.
Karachi, Baghdad, and Homs.
Ankara calling.

Golden State—Cleveland.
Each three-pointer from downtown
a globe in freefall.

Sasha, Malia
whisked off in an Escalade,
their faces looming.

Denver. Sandy Hook.
Charleston, and then Orlando.
More lives, more coffins.

And somewhere far off
a predator drone launches
its dark, furtive flight.

## MR. KHAN

The Bengali at the corner liquor store
who counts out change on my weekend six-pack,
and yet whose name I cannot actually recall
despite it sounding suspiciously similar

to the Pakistani doctor threading a catheter
up through my mother's groin to the aorta,
carrying with it the replacement bovine valve
he deploys to save her, as the Hindu nurse

monitors vitals on a screen whose software
was long ago designed by a Kashmiri Muslim
now hoping, praying for his Catholic grandson
to return home stateside, maybe by the playoffs

so together they can watch the Yankees explode,
the crowd-careening frenzy and sirens set off,
all of us at home ensconced like pashas,
the diehard faithful patiently keeping score.

# BLOOD MOON BLUES

protesters marched
shutting down cities
senators sponsored
their own annuities

car bombs were back
hem lines higher
forecasters tracked
low fronts and fires

children were told
their parents were thugs
governments banned
playgrounds and hugs

analysts mourned
stagnating markets
terrorists surveyed
expanded new targets

refugees crossed
invisible borders
arriving malnourished
colder and poorer

high up above
a blood moon rose
the seas churned on
the shore decomposed

Venus and Mars
ascended in unison
glaciers kept forming
palatial ruins

while higher yet
at the back of space
a star imploded
leaving no trace

but hydrogen and helium
the seeds of our genus
potent as love
or a neutral virus

# FACIAL RECOGNITION

when they come for you
you will recognize them
by their vacant eyes
imprinted provinces
of residual fear

turned cold retaliation
harboring the just
barely sustained
conviction to deport
themselves as legal

witnesses who will attest
to the mother's heaving
collateral sobs you cuffed
and the child the man
who knows you now

# NOBODY'S ROAD

Nobody knows what troubled the kid.
Nobody even knew where he lived.

Nobody remembers hearing a thing.
Nobody considered inquiring.

Nobody thought to call the police.
Nobody worried it would come to this.

Nobody can say how he got inside.
Nobody knows yet how many died.

Nobody can think of just what to do.
Nobody can help but feel déjà vu.

Nobody agrees how to prevent it.
Nobody wants their rights suspended.

Nobody can fathom the depth of such grief.
Nobody is sure just what to believe.

Nobody can undo what has been done.
Nobody is watching the neighbor's son.

# TO THE COMING DISASTER

somewhere in the heart of Texas
a small town explodes is thankful
on camera God was watching

classmates dead or stunned
a live feed streaming captives
unable to verify casualties

we leave you with this story
caught on tape sequestered
imprisoned smuggled released

# II

# AUBADE

the seagull
kiting
in a cage
of wind

navigates
again
its scry
of need

beyond
the docks
the wooden boats
rough

barbs
buoying
flight
toward an end

to flight
and gravity
riding
the wind

# LITTLE PROBLEM

longing we say
and by extension
imply duration
we cannot stay

caught as we are
somewhere between
the all apparent
and what we've seen

of storms of harbors
the wind-chopped bay
laced with whitecaps
like macramé

slow to unravel
and tattered seem
knotted with longing
we cannot stay

# ASHORE

## MAP

where we are going
it isn't clear
since where we are
is already here

aware the far shore
is a bit more near
than first expected
or was made clear

by starlight guiding
the course we steer
blithely upon
the cusp of fear

of never knowing
that it's clear
where we are going
is already here

## SURVEY

*How deep is the lake?*
As deep as it gets.
*Who dammed the river?*
Nobody yet.

*Which way runs the current?*
Both east and west.
*Can you swim in it?*
Try your best.

*Has anyone ever drowned?*
A few, not all.
*Are there any fish in it?*
Large and small.

*What is its name?*
"Kettle" in Mahican.
*How long has it been here?*
A day and an eon.

*Does it ever freeze over?*
Absent the sun.
*How long have you lived here?*
The water flows on . . .

## CENSUS

fishermen on the lake
make no mistake
and cast their line ashore

fishermen on the shore
want something more
and strike the hidden middle

the wide water waits
mysterious and calm
its depths built for drowning

its surface always level

# WILLOW

amid the toss
of light that rakes
the rust of oak
pearl gray
cloud cover
bellying rain

the willow lingers

pliant with weeping
that is not there
and yet is what
we know it by
among hemlock
among ash

beside the lake

water that laps
the rocky shore
as a heron unfolds
its pageant slate
above the surface
rippling bruise

# RAIN

falling and falling
cannot be
a curse of becoming
the blight of day

aqueous free
to trample hay
cut for winter
or left to rot

fields ferns
fog-bound weather
perpetual as air
or an Ararat

# SOLSTICE

that on this day
of winter dark
rain impelling
the ribbed coppery
flash of oak leaves

the year should end
and compel the mind
toward the gravity
of pines tremulous
with wind hail blast

and a moment marked
as the sun draws farthest
away from the earth
and seems to pause
before returning

# NADIR

out of the air
    the air embodied
settles as flurries
    down laden streets

soft declamations
    of silence unhurried
earthward their journey
    emptied of wind

lake ice contracting
    its vice of cold
murmured music
    on which we skate

# NARCISSI

forced in February
six-petaled stars
crown these airy
tall columnar

stems inclining
their heavy heads—
weary pining
for a death attended

not by the tremor
of papery husks
but star-lit verdure
at winter's dusk

## CREDO

never complain
the jonquils say
blowzy with breeze
they cannot hold

and the breeze itself
—saturated, cold—
dispenses torrents
a black cloud drained

to quick exhaustion
and the marauded plain
of jonquils blazoned
—never complain

# NOCTURNE

suffice it to say
the full moon's
hard light exposing
the ambush of sea
invading the harbor

cannot know
the concerted blast
that cripples an elm
to a stack of limbs—
suffice

it to say
and say it to praise
the burnished horizon
its collar of rust
suppliant above

the sea's reckless glitter
these meager stars
piercing the scrim
of moonlight proffered
its silver its peace

# III

# WATER LILIES

*Claude Monet, 1917*

Meanwhile, he painted them—lilies
floating on the surface of a pond
he'd constructed "for the pleasure of the eye
and motifs to paint" at century's end,
the new one begun with multiple explosions
of carmine, coral, white fleshy flowers
against the backdrop of a subsurface blue

with distances, the sky stretched out
upon the watery calm where a cloudy puff
would later be captured by his brush
in motion, each day in the studio
another one spent to the echo of guns
bombarding the trenches, pummeling the Somme,
erupting in billows of char-black smoke

beyond a horizon no longer present
but subsumed, erased, immersed as he was
in the flux of light on water, flowers
astride turbid shallows beneath a willow
and its weeping, our only perspective
in a lost world lost to bottomless translucency,
the eye that sees it, and the intractable sun.

# LANDSCAPE

*for Katharina Prantl*

earth water and sky
the sky upended
earth unbound
by water the sky
now breathing now
upon this earth
its cave of splendor
of sky on water
rooted in the blue
insuperable green
this whir this
quickening

# SUN THROUGH SNOW

Turner could have done no better,
nor did he, articulating the light
made now radiant, prismatic:
hills, lake, trees, and woolen sky
filtered by this sun-threaded squall
of snow as real as veneration,

the smell of rain, the heft of stone,
or the thought that within an hour
it will be gone, the veer and waft
and thrust of clouds and light
electric with the backlit pulse
and shimmer of each ray of snow

consigned to memory and weather
closing down this moment's glow.

# SOUNDBOARD

When Archie told me the incredible story
of Lady Margaret's piano, an Obermeier plucked
from a forgotten warehouse in bombed-out Berlin,
then secretly carted off, scarfed up by the Allies
and loaded onto a plane, delivered to Ireland
only to end up the elaborate inlaid soundboard
holding Peg's ashtray, her snooker of gin,

simply amazed, I couldn't stop thinking
of Pasternak's piano tossed from a window,
workmen at his dacha deeming it worthless
decades after his death and the poem he wrote
that warned his lover, "The shivering piano
will discompose you. . . . Death is in the air.
One opens up one's veins much like a window."

# HAPPY TRAILS

Thirty-five years ago,
one night in a Dublin hostel,
Dostoevsky on my pillow
beneath a 40-watt bulb,

trying to forget the sound
of young Fiona Magee,
diabetic, wheelchair bound,
a double amputee,

squealing through paper walls,
"Ah, couldn't ye love him so!"
the reply, something inaudible,
thirty-five years ago.

# THE WILD BOAR

Was it Kiki or Heinz who offered us
that ride at dusk from Hamburg to Berlin
those many years ago, the sun setting across
the barren expanse of a North Sea march
as the car (an out-of-service ambulance)
pulled onto the transit highway from which
there was no getting off except to stop,

wait for the East German cops to show up
and question the driver and his passengers
as to why we'd halted the car and delayed
our scheduled arrival in Berlin, surrounded
as we were by borderless frozen fields
vacant as the eyes of that policeman
unable, or at least unwilling, to believe

we'd hit something in the dark which—bang!—
was there and gone, the driver turning
onto the gravel shoulder as we got out
to assess the damage done, the headlight
shattered and caved in, while at the edge,
caught in the twisted chrome and there
for the cop to inspect, the bristles of a boar

we'd hit which none of us could see
or saw as it crossed into our path
all those years ago, the wind slicing
through us, that transit highway bleak
as the thought of tomorrow among
the closed-off reaches where that boar still ran,
wounded and mortal—was it Gabi? was it Fritz?

# LATE ELEGY FOR SEAMUS HEANEY

## I

The tide was out at Sandymount
that day I strolled atop its muddy sheen,
Sugarloaf's peaked point a toppled lyre
down Wicklow way, dogs shed of leashes
racing the strand in tongue-lolling ecstasy,
while around me head-bent, mindful joggers
strapped to iPods powered on through
the weekend's reprieve from another week.

The tide was low, as I said, not wishing to
repeat myself, and yet unable to check
the odd feel of forty years returning
through a door left ajar, passed by, still
open to spirits moving in and out at will,
communing, whispering from the throaty dark.

## II

The Martello Tower, fortified in prose
of a higher order in Joyce's version,
still stands squat, staring down the cove
and those gravid breakers advancing
on decommissioned cannon disappeared
and never fired. Reticent, bog flown,
the prevailing wind is westerly, more cool
than raw, a ladleful of well in summer.

But this is January, memory and its tricks
gone topsy-turvy like the clouds adrift
mirrored tide pools that punctuate the beach,
mother-of-pearl pots brim-full with sky
more nimbus than cumulus, more storm
than bits of sun flashing at my feet.

## III

Traffic along the strand road has grown
incorrigible, Ireland and dirty Dublin
conquered again, this time by double glazing.
Stockpiles of fresh green glass financed
by financing rise beneath tall beaky cranes
whose silent sweep plucks straw girders
to lace the nests of those hungry to invest
far more in futures than a turf-dug past.

Supple, smoky, lifting from a field
with a raptor's weighty flight, your voice
back then was confraternal, yet of its own
element pointed toward a true north,
opening the present amid the fallow ground
of history's alluvium, its buried bones.

## IV

I hardly knew you, but somehow I did,
just like so many others made familiar
and local to landscapes imagined amid
the bodhrán beat of your meter's timbre
drumming its hailstones on slate roofs slick,
a hayloft's dank confessional, the chiseled strike
revealing the coal block's diamond black
interior converted to staying warmth within

the irrefutable vernacular
that was your lodestone's ionic draw
attracting, collecting, defining its fundamental
faith in the aura of things, each day's
chaff and rain-rinsed heft made unimpeachable,
not the moving target of a loaded gun.

## V

Place was your working canvas, though travel
and honorifics dispensed you to the industry
of others championing the primal cause: poetry
birthed in a Derry cowshed—linear, clear
as a silver contrail arrowing the salt blue
empyrean above the Atlantic's chop
still vaulted by a currach's wave-beaten measure,
the thin air of celebrity your final stop,

but not your resting. No, no, it was place:
Mossbawn, Belfast, Wicklow, the siloed aerie
of the study in Sandymount, a pen nib's river
quietly inking Sweeney's mad journey
that never left its source, the green country
of the spirit freed and spoken, at last voiced.

## VI

So say it, say it here in Dublintown,
write it in the sand of Sandymount Beach,
the life you lived is alive and remains
in syllables set down, their earthen reach
like veins of ore beneath the loamy dark,
or a DART's reflexive shudder speeding past
lowered gates that lift then like a prayer
to passing through and the sea-bright air

that floods their wake with a pungent whiff
of cockles and razor clams dotting the strand
old couples amble through like memory,
as children raise a kite, myself word heavy
and muttering to the waves now rolling in,
unmoored, yet anchored, unafraid.

# ANNAGHMAKERRIG

I'm taking with me
three chestnuts found
at Annaghmakerrig

chuckling like stones
inside the pocket
of a meadow stream

on the far shore
where whooper paddle
the shallow inlet

grebes and pintails
nestle inside
a reed bed's blind

and rain mist
like a bellows
flutters the surface

of wind wet shining
dark chestnuts polished
at Annaghmakerrig

# EPIPHANY

I wish I could write like Michael Longley,
flower-besotted at Carrigskeewaun,
where the birds' winged monikers still hover
—*chiffchaff, whimbrel, curlew, sanderling*—
near tide pools awash with otters foraging
mollusks and snails to the peep of plovers
skittering sea reach on slick-back sand,

and not this grab bag of eagles, muskrats,
the heron's slate stillness unbending to strike
quick as a thought the length of pickerel
now threading the dark of its S-curve gullet,
a wad of cash in an old crone's bedroll,
the heron a woodcut—motionless epiphany . . .
I wish I could write like Michael Longley.

## POEM

ice on a rain filled barrel
            a penumbra
of swollen gun cotton sky
            absolving snow
to bury the inflected
            reflected flakes falling
upon a chill mirror
            buoyed in the barrel
by rain swallowed light

# IV

# CROWS

all afternoon
crows caw
their oracular
dark music
through pine

twilight
snow softening
sharp edges
of guttural
crow talk

# AUGURY

Orion's sword glints in a sky gone platinum
as winter cuts its teeth on a bone-white moon.
Oak leaves, frozen, tremble like seraphim
mauled by a gale whose tin-whistle tune
strips the season of its last live harvest,
scattering windfalls like abandoned ballast.

November. Midnight. Soon the Geminids
will fade as portents reduced to rumor,
as gravity takes hold, mortals and demigods
tempted to read in each burnt-out meteor
reprieve or good omen traversing the skies.
The planet spins on. The oceans rise.

# FALSE CARDINAL

Just before sunset a cardinal sets
its *doo-wop-chirp-chirp* atop an elm,
a knot of flame like an epithet
inside the evening's sky-blue dome.

Spring again, the cardinal's return
now three weeks early, revenant
of a future we've come to learn
will see the planet dead and spent

or not, or maybe so, while likely
the cardinal's song, undulant still
in its late-day-last-call reveille,

will find us at evening facing west,
transfixed and emblazoned, a cardinal
sun sinking in each pane of glass.

# FORECAST

the light will harden
on church spires lacquered
like glassy stalagmites

aglare with the heat
no longer a spell
but volcanic instead

lava's long slow
locomotive reach
a swollen stalled high

oozing its ozone
breathless as fossils
fueled by old age

rain a remnant
stippling fields
awash in ash

# COCKLES

sweet as abandon
an inlet's palette
muscled plankton
amorphous gullet

swallowing eons
in a grain of beach
ribbed origin
wombed reach

cribbed by sand
nursed on brine
heart clam
a bay's hard coin

splayed on a plate
bibbed with lettuce
mouths agape
the glut of status

washing them down
with vintage swill
fat meaty mounds
mute mandibles

## ARROWHEAD

flint point planted
in moraine gravel
each beveled chink
a milk-gray ghost
Mohawk? Mahican?

there is no nation
to water's chuffed
sun-voweled surface
or the indolent trout
ashine and spotted

as an arrow aims
shoots pierces wild
hunger gutted
in the silver sheen
of limp wet fish

the chalk-dry taste
of history
in the arrowhead
that lies askant
my narrow desk

# THE TOAD

When I was five or six (not yet ten),
I stumbled across a toad inside our garden,
hunkered under squash leaves branching out,
a camouflage ceiling protecting the green
bloated body, its warty snout
and ink-black eyes whose oily sheen
reflected back a timid tiny hand
that grabbed it, hurled it, aiming to land

it and obliterate it against a tree
next to our garden, looming over me
at the edge of crooked rows and weedy beds
inspecting a sodden corpse, a pulverated head
before me now still thinking back to then
when I was five or six, or maybe ten.

# THE BASS

At the height of summer,
suspended beneath the calm,
the hulk of bass sat breathing
and did not move or flinch.

Thinking it a cinch,
we grabbed a ragged net,
angled our shadows
over the dock's rough edge,

and jabbed and yelped
at the heaving weight
of bass bent doubled up,
thrashing the garish light—

and knew the taste of violation
in the empty shock of air,
like a thirst for love or freedom,
like a wound beyond repair.

Until we let it go,
there in our muggy stupor,
as it bolted the folds
of the grainy water.

# ORACLE

We look to nature for what we long to see,
a cloud's dissembled face in the aqua blue,
the reed-buffeting breeze, the slow shamble
of water chuckling the creek bed's gravel.

Whatever is hidden at a glance's edge
the mind will have it—a bobcat spotting prey
too far outside its burrow's sunken cavern,
the spider stalking a fly in the nimbus of a web,

the owl's muffled flight, the pewter gleam
of a muddy river's eel, the tympani of ice
thrumming a lake's black kettle—marginalia
in motion within this evening's pregnant calm

are palpable yet invisible, magnified
dark silhouetted hills dilating before you,
dusk sharpening their backlit ridges,
talismans at twilight, the whir of birds.

# STARLINGS

starlings at sunset
hurtle the cove
higgledy-piggledy
to roost a dead elm

corpuscles of dusk
against a twilight
receding like a thought
I cannot remember

amid ratchety *jeeeers*
from a far shore

# FOR THE BIRDS

Starlings don't know they are starlings
*jeeeering* at sunset atop a dead elm,
nor crows their intricate gutturals
as crow talk at dawn, while even mute swans
crossing a pond sotto voce in autumn
are strangers themselves to that silent bevy
of white C clefs we recognize as *swan*.

And yet by extension, when you think of it,
neither does the wayward birder
stalking a lesser greenlet in its green den,
or trickier, much harder to see
among the blue unhurried wash of summer
those far-off choruses of trills and whistles,
peeps and mewings, high hovering *keeer-r-r*.

## TURTLE

*for N. H., in memoriam*

Shy panzer of the swamp, atavistic
in your haughty calm, you blink at us
encapsulated in our swanky Prius,
crossing the road from the prehistoric

world you're going to or coming from
to lay your eggs in the sandy bed
of tomorrow, knowing like the dead
that, however slow, it indeed will come.

And does, even if absent of you—
sanguine, curmudgeonly, immemorial
as mud, or the memory of mud

propelling you on as you cling to
your path through fan-tailed ferns that flood
our eyes with green heraldry, fresh and real.

# V

If there is not another life,
there is at least another way to live.

Theodore Roethke, from *Straw for the Fire: From the Notebooks of Theodore Roethke, 1943–1963*

# WRITINGS

swallows at daybreak—
pure inviolate sounds
the flit and splutter
of their antic rounds

across lake glass
dipping their tails
mid-flight and lambent
translucent inkwells

left pooled and pooling
toward the outer shore
a water-pocked trail
their signature

# MOONLIGHT

elvers on water
pixelate silver
sheen undulating
a transfixed retina

aswim with the music
of this August sonata
whose score plays out
a silence broken

only by mouthfuls
churned by fishtails
wet muggy gulps
of platinum air

# BOLDINI'S CATCH

*Giovanni Boldini, 1879*

Safely ashore, Boldini's catch is in:
anchor planted among the clatter of rocks,
the villagers crowd around, lost to the din
of fishwife and monger arguing the cost
of the day's live haul—conger teeming in vats
we do not see, but sense, perhaps imagine,
subject as we are to this Êtretat
composed of canvas, pigment, oil, and resin
awash with sea brine, mottled light that swells
with the gull's far cry and an ocean's smell.

## SHELL

held to the ear
there's nothing to hear
but what's not there

as somewhere
the roar
crashes ashore

on the cochlear
coast of the concha's weir
of atmosphere

# AT ANCHOR

*for Lynn and Jeff Callahan*

*Alchemy*, *Cirrus*, *Mockingbird*, *Rogue*,
vesseled monikers within whose hold
fortune's swells and eddies rest
temporarily contemporaneous,

*Pot o' Gold* and *Down n' Out*
as like as *Revelation* to flout
brassy pretense above *Enigma*'s dinghy,
while *Solitude* heads once more to sea.

What's in a name? *Juliet* might know,
but she's not telling. *Ivanhoe*
and *Rhumba*, *Magic Jack*, and *Djinn*,
all incarnations of whatever whim

set them afloat upon those tides
of money, romance, or sporting pride
which land *Bess* in a thirty-knot squall,
or another case of caviar on *Iron Will*.

All is *Happenstance*, all *Illusion*,
or is it? *Loss*, *Pain*, *Utter Confusion*,
just where are they? Scuttled, no doubt,
*Failure*, *Termites*, *Cancer*, *Gout*

banned as well by deference? custom?
or those leveling humors that steer us home
to one another, stranded as we are
in a sea of signs and seeking harbor

in the quiet smile that understands
*Divorce* a sly nod at *Vindication*
for some, *True Hearts* but rarely true
for others, while those on *Missing You*

at anchor within that sun-pooling cove
must plunder memory to find their love
present and accounted for, albeit gone,
as a buoy bells out its constant song.

Meanwhile, with *Distraction* out at sea,
*Invictus* loses again to *Destiny*,
as its captain curses that tub *Cantata*
for cutting him off in the annual regatta,

thus costing his name etched in pewter
polished to hold the somber luster
of the harbor at twilight, *That's My Hon'*
sunk in the shadow of the cutter *Python*.

# O

As the deaf-mute grocery clerk
puckers curious to a chorus "O"
to ask what kind of mushrooms
he should be ringing up, I think

of Ortiz and last night's double
sailing like a lit-up vowel
toward the bleachers in center-left,
the outfielder unsure if it might

carry The Monster or carom off
when, in fact, it hits the warning
track, goes dead, toppling the fielder

decisively into the dirt, Ortiz
on second, me mouthing "oyster"
to the far reaches of the Mystic Big Y.

# THE HOURS

## MATINS

in the indicative dark
somber houses
stand preoccupied

by moonlight
implicating the elms
upon their surfaces

so many thin arms
raised in hallelujahs
inking hard shadows

## LAUDS

the stars unload
their narratives
of dust

the moon a prayer
its fullness exuding
light that shines

from arid plains
craters awash
in tranquility

PRIME

and the ascension
of the planets
swift wheeling

constellations
crosses the sky
to empty out

the geography
of night into
the visible

TERCE

all over town
the drift and sheer
of daylight untangles

down from a poplar
on the scatter of wind
disseminating white

angels that clutch
gray seeds
of hosannas

## SEXT

among the clatter
of dishes and daydreams
served up at the diner

ghostly steam
slowly unfurls
above coffee

cups lifting
black votives
of thirst

## NONES

a buzzard picks
at the flesh
of a pigeon

as cars circle
the village green
and the gorging

still rapture
of hungry raptor
quietly feeding

## VESPERS

toward evening
toward night a
setting things

down toward
evening the wide
open spaces

traffic
exhaling its
halo of sighs

## COMPLINE

and the moon
again risen
traces its arc

to excavate
the quiet of
houses unloading

their amber
soft veils
printing the lawns

## A SOFT DAY

Lovely the soft day
when hours stretch like months,
as out a window one's gaze
hurdles entanglements

of love or work or health,
and we recall what we see
is a cloud whose subtle stealth
belies a threnody

more mist than drizzle,
a wet muffled murmur
moist as a kettle's whistle,
hard rain a distant rumor

yet here and still composed of
salving dew on fresh cut grass,
saturate gray air that floats above
a subdued susurration, a damp excess.

# MAKING HAY

*for R. W., in memoriam*

Dotting a fresh mown pasture
they are abstracted—
lozenges of green whose yield
will feed a winter's hunger
with a summer's field.

For now they sit there,
circumspect and salient
as totems to another time
whose sickles and scythes
ceded the baler's tines

this sun-baked stubbled plain
of timothy and fescue
configured with each pass,
summer materialized
in cylinders of grass.

Yet, absent the sharp inflections
of blade on polished hone,
is there really any loss?
Or is it dim nostalgia
denying *is* for *was?*

For it's haying that remains,
patient mindful husbandry
never quite out of style,
so long as the scent of clover
still carries a country mile

to circulate among us
lost to screens and pixels
the freshet of this summer day,
sweet with its own idiom:
the musk-green smell of hay.

# DAY IN, DAY OUT

## 1

The lag and slow and lazy snug of it.
Rain pattering the roof, house lights on
at 10 a.m., the day itself a clarion
call to nothing but the indigent
wastes of folly, curlicues of dream
emitted from a second cup of tea
next to an open book, clemency
in the air and the clank of steam
pipes forging an anchored sense
of habitation, pearl-dripping eaves
measuring time like a metronome
or that *partita*, its mind-clearing lens
radioed in on the pulse of static heaves
surging like stormfall on the shore of home.

## II

The blizzard shut down the road to school
but not our restless spirits, booted and ready
to get on out there and get it built,
the snow fort gouged out shovelful
by shovelful inside a mountainous drift
until, dug in, well-armed, we felt it safe
to launch our synchronized offensive
on another fort, then await the *szzz*
and *whomp* of those missiles pelting fast
as snowflakes later mixing with the sleet
on an unplowed back road, headlights
iced over, the storm an ambush of white
I had to battle through in order to meet
the porchlight on and waiting, home at last.

### III

Once more the day's particulars: the lake
a scrub of whitecaps beneath cloud cover,
blast waves of wind, a wall of rain
causing the house to creak and shake
like no tomorrow, which in fact is true
for the one who, at the desk and lamp-lit,
rides out each hour's warp and weft
of iteration, plummeting what he knew
in order to know it again, yet different.
Like someone lost in a snowfield, circling
back on his tracks. Like a train that shudders
when swept by another from where it's bent.
Like safe harbor found in a three-day storm
by a fitful wooden schooner making for home.

# ENVOY

*for Abbot Cutler*

A burl of light on a pane-glass window;
cold drizzle, wet snow, eruptive weather.

And this our only legacy—to know
the low-hung cloud that glances off
a mirrored surface yet more real
than the cloud itself, muddy April
indecisive to the last, mimicking

the slap of wipers back and forth
across the slope of windshield,
or oddly at the corner of Main & North
that storefront window reflecting now
the curve of heaven, the noxious exhaust,

pedestrians astride the polished glass,
the cars rolling by, the dog on its leash.

## NOTES ON THE POEMS

The epigraphs that appear on p. ix and p. 67 are taken from *Straw for the Fire: From the Notebooks of Theodore Roethke, 1943–1963*, selected and arranged by David Wagoner (New York: Anchor/Doubleday, 1974).

"Uterine Vellum": The two-line quotation that ends the poem is an adaptation from a sentence in William Horman's *Vulgaria* (1519). Special thanks to Mark Richards for informing me about the niceties of uterine vellum.

"Augustine's Vision": The quotation that appears in the penultimate stanza is from Augustine's *Order in the Universe* as cited by Garry Wills in his biography *Saint Augustine: A Life* (New York: Viking Penguin, 1999).

"Solstice": The closing lines follow the definition of the winter solstice found in *Funk & Wagnalls Standard College Dictionary* (New York: Harcourt Brace, 1966).

"Water Lilies": The quotation is from Monet's 1893 letter to the municipal authorities of Giverny asking for permission to divert water from the river Epte in order to create a pond for aquatic plants. It is cited in Michel Hoog's *Nymphéas of Claude Monet at the Musée de l'Orangerie*, translated by Jean-Marie Clarke (Paris: Réunion des Musées Nationaux, 1990).

"Soundboard": The lines attributed to Boris Pasternak are adapted from his poem titled "The shiv'ring piano, foaming at the mouth," which appears in an anonymous English translation on allpoetry.com.

"Late Elegy for Seamus Heaney": DART stands for Dublin Area Rapid Transit.

"Boldini's Catch": The painting referred to is titled *The Return of the Fishing Boats, Étretat* (1879), and is located at the Sterling and Francine Clark Art Institute in Williamstown, MA.

## ACKNOWLEDGMENTS

*My thanks to the editors of the following periodicals in which the poems listed have been published, some of them in slightly different form:*

| | |
|---|---|
| *The American Scholar* | "Water Lilies, "Poem" |
| *The Common* | "Sun Through Snow," "O,"<br>"Triptych," "The Hours" |
| *Fulcrum Annual* | "Augustine's Vision" |
| *The Hopkins Review* | "Happy Trails,"<br>"To the Coming Disaster" |
| *Narrative* | "The Wild Boar" |
| *The New Criterion* | "Making Hay" |
| *Oxidant/Engine* | "Facial Recognition" |
| *The Paris Review* | "Soundboard" |
| *Provincetown Arts* | "Cockles" |
| *Salmagundi* | "Auden's Glasses,"<br>"The Hitler Bug" |
| *The Sewanee Review* | "Day In, Day Out," "Envoy" |
| *Subtropics* | "Shell" |
| *The Yale Review* | "Little Problem," "Credo" |

"Water Lilies," "The Wild Boar," and "Augustine's Vision" appeared in the chapbook *Augustine's Vision* (New American Press, 2010).

"Shell" was reprinted in *The Winter Anthology,* Volume 4. "Nobody's Road" was broadcast as an online link to the February 21, 2013 broadcast of the PBS show *Need to Know* that discussed gun violence after the 2012 Newtown shooting.

I also wish to thank the MacDowell Colony, the James Merrill House, and the Tyrone Guthrie Centre for valuable residencies during which many of these poems were begun. Thanks as well to Bard College at Simon's Rock for a sabbatical leave that allowed for this book's completion. Deepest gratitude goes out to John Hennessy, John Koethe, Wyatt Prunty, Susan Roeper, Vijay Seshadri, and Rosanna Warren for their invaluable comments and suggestions along the way.

## ABOUT THE AUTHOR

Peter Filkins is the author of four previous collections of poetry: *What She Knew*, *After Homer*, *Augustine's Vision*, and *The View We're Granted*, for which he received the 2013 Sheila Margaret Motton Book Prize from the New England Poetry Club. His work has received the Stover Memorial Award in Poetry from *Southwest Review*, the New American Press Chapbook Award, a Finalist Award in Poetry from the Mass Cultural Council, an Outstanding Translation Award from the American Literary Translators Association, a Berlin Prize from the American Academy in Berlin, and residencies at the MacDowell Colony, Yaddo, the Millay Colony, the James Merrill House, and the Tyrone Guthrie Centre. His poems, essays, and translations have appeared in the *American Scholar*, the *New Republic*, *Poetry*, the *Yale Review*, the *Sewanee Review*, the *Paris Review*, the *New York Times Book Review*, and numerous other publications. He serves as the Richard B. Fisher Professor of Literature & Creative Writing at Bard College at Simon's Rock and also teaches translation at Bard's main campus in Annandale-on-Hudson

## POETRY TITLES IN THE SERIES

John Hollander,
*Blue Wine and Other Poems*

Robert Pack,
*Waking to My Name: New and Selected Poems*

Philip Dacey,
*The Boy under the Bed*

Wyatt Prunty,
*The Times Between*

Barry Spacks,
*Spacks Street, New and Selected Poems*

Gibbons Ruark,
*Keeping Company*

David St. John,
*Hush*

Wyatt Prunty,
*What Women Know, What Men Believe*

Adrien Stoutenberg,
*Land of Superior Mirages: New and Selected Poems*

John Hollander,
*In Time and Place*

Charles Martin,
*Steal the Bacon*

John Bricuth,
*The Heisenberg Variations*

Tom Disch,
*Yes, Let's: New and Selected Poems*

Wyatt Prunty,
*Balance as Belief*

Tom Disch,
*Dark Verses and Light*

Thomas Carper,
*Fiddle Lane*

Emily Grosholz,
*Eden*

X. J. Kennedy,
*Dark Horses: New Poems*

Wyatt Prunty,
*The Run of the House*

Robert Phillips,
*Breakdown Lane*

Vicki Hearne,
*The Parts of Light*

Timothy Steele,
*The Color Wheel*

Josephine Jacobsen,
*In the Crevice of Time: New and Collected Poems*

Thomas Carper,
*From Nature*

John Burt,
*Work without Hope: Poetry by John Burt*

Charles Martin,
*What the Darkness Proposes: Poems*

Wyatt Prunty,
*Since the Noon Mail Stopped*

William Jay Smith,
*The World below the Window: Poems 1937–1997*

Wyatt Prunty,
*Unarmed and Dangerous: New and Selected Poems*

Robert Phillips,
*Spinach Days*

X. J. Kennedy,
*The Lords of Misrule: Poems 1992–2001*

John T. Irwin, ed.,
*Words Brushed by Music: Twenty-Five Years of the Johns Hopkins Poetry Series*

John Bricuth,
*As Long As It's Big: A Narrative Poem*

Robert Phillips,
*Circumstances Beyond Our Control: Poems*

Daniel Anderson,
*Drunk in Sunlight*

X. J. Kennedy,
*In a Prominent Bar in Secaucus: New and Selected Poems, 1955–2007*

William Jay Smith,
*Words by the Water*

Wyatt Prunty,
*The Lover's Guide to Trapping*

Charles Martin,
*Signs & Wonders*

Peter Filkins,
*The View We're Granted*

Brian Swann,
*In Late Light*

Daniel Anderson,
*The Night Guard at the Wilberforce Hotel*

Wyatt Prunty,
*Couldn't Prove, Had to Promise*

John Bricuth,
*Pure Products of America, Inc.*

X. J. Kennedy,
*That Swing: Poems 2008–2016*

Charles Martin,
*Future Perfect*

Hastings Hensel,
*Ballyhoo*

Sidney Wade,
*Deep Gossip*

Peter Filkins,
*Water / Music*

Printed in the USA
CPSIA information can be obtained
at www.ICGtesting.com
CBHW032350031224
18411CB00030B/537

9 781421 440088